contents

NZ, Canada, US and UK readers
Please note that Australian cup and spoon measurements are metric. A conversion chart appears on page 63.

ingredients from a thai kitchen

baby eggplants also known as Japanese eggplant, these are small and slender. They don't need to be salted before use.

bamboo shoots the tender shoots of bamboo plants; available in cans.

bean thread noodles also called cellophane noodles or bean thread vermicelli; made from green mung bean flour.

chillies, red thai also called birdseye chillies, these tiny chillies are very hot and well suited to drying.

chinese cabbage also known as peking cabbage or napa cabbage; has crisp texture and milder flavour than common cabbage.

coconut cream the first pressing from grated mature coconut and water.

coconut milk the second pressing (less rich) from grated mature coconut.

coriander

dried: coriander seeds and ground coriander taste very different to fresh coriander.

fresh: also known as cilantro and chinese parsley; in Thai food, the whole plant is used – leaves, stems and roots.

galangal looks like ginger but is dense, fibrous and harder to cut. Galangal has a distinctive flavour; if using pieces, remove before serving.

pickled: also known as ka dong; sold in cryovac packs or in jars in Asian grocery stores. You can substitute pickled ginger, but the taste will differ.

ginger also known as green or root ginger.

pickled: sweet and pink, and available in jars from specialty Asian food stores.

green curry paste available ready-made in supermarkets, or turn to page 61 for the recipe.

green peppercorns, pickled have a herbal flavour; early-harvested unripe pepper. We used Thai green peppercorns, canned in clusters, but you can use green peppercorns in brine.

fish sauce also called nam pla or nuoc nam; made from pulverised, salted, fermented fish. Has pungent smell and strong taste.

jasmine rice aromatic long-grain white rice.

ka chai sometimes spelled krachai or kah chi, also known as lesser galangal, chinese ginger or finger-root; long, fingerling-like roots available fresh, dried, canned or pickled. Similar flavour to ginger; purchase in Asian specialty stores.

kaffir lime leaves thick leaves that impart a strong citrus flavour. Dried leaves are also available; add these to curries.

kumara Polynesian name of orange-fleshed sweet potato often confused with yam.

lemon grass a tall, clumping, lemon-smelling and -tasting, sharp-edged grass; the white lower part of the stem is used in cooking.

lychees delicious juicy fruit; red-skinned, white-fleshed with a black seed. Also available canned in syrup.

massaman curry paste available ready-made in supermarkets, or turn to page 60 for recipe.

oil, peanut pressed from ground peanuts; most common oil in Asian cooking due to its high smoke point.

palm sugar also known as jaggery, jawa and gula melaka; from the coconut palm. Dark brown in colour; sold in rock-hard cakes.

panang curry paste available ready-made in supermarkets, or turn to page 61 for recipe.

papaya, green available in various sizes at many Asian shops and markets; should be hard, shiny and completely unripe, the flesh so light green in colour it is almost white.

pea eggplants slightly larger than a green pea and a similar shape and colour; sold fresh, in bunches, or pickled in jars. Thai eggplant can be used as a substitute; purchase in Asian grocery stores.

pomelos similar to grapefruit but sweeter, more conical in shape and slightly larger.

red curry paste available ready-made in supermarkets, or see page 60 for recipe.

rice stick noodles available in varying thicknesses; also known as rice vermicelli. Soak in boiling water to soften, but test often as they can turn mushy.

rice vermicelli also known as mei fun or bee hoon; similar to bean thread vermicelli but longer and made with rice flour.

sambal oelek (also ulek or olek) a salty paste made from ground chillies.

snake beans thin, long (about 40cm), fresh green beans, with similar taste to green beans. Also called yard-long beans.

shallots, fried usually served sprinkled over just-cooked dishes. Available at Asian grocery stores.

shrimp paste also known as trasi and blachan; almost solid preserved paste made of salted dried shrimp.

shrimp, dried available at Asian food stores; once opened, store in refrigerator.

star anise a dried star-shaped pod used to impart an astringent aniseed flavour.

tamarind

concentrate: (or paste) a thick, purple-black paste extracted from pulp of tamarind bean; used to impart a sour flavour.

dried: dried blocks of tamarind pulp and seeds, from pod of the tamarind tree; available in Asian food stores.

thai basil also known as horapa; different from holy basil and sweet basil in look and taste. Having smaller leaves and purplish stems, it has a slight licorice or aniseed taste.

thai eggplant golf-ball size eggplants available in different colours, but most commonly green traced in off-white.

thai shallots, purple (homm) also called asian or pink shallots; a member of the onion family but resemble garlic in that they grow in multiple-clove bulbs and are intensely flavoured.

tofu also known as bean curd; a bland, slightly nutty food made from soy bean "milk". Available from supermarkets; once opened, store in refrigerator in water for a few days at most, changing the water daily.

firm: this has been pressed slightly; it holds its shape and can be cut into cubes.

silken: custard-like, soft tofu.

turmeric this root is available fresh or dried and ground, resulting in a yellow powder.

vietnamese mint a pungent and peppery narrow-leafed member of the buckwheat family. It is also known as cambodian mint, pak pai or laksa leaf.

yellow curry paste available ready-made in supermarkets, or turn to page 61 for recipe.

spring rolls

20g rice vermicelli
2 teaspoons peanut oil
100g pork mince
1 clove garlic, crushed
1 fresh red thai chilli,
    chopped finely
1 green onion, chopped finely
1 small carrot (70g),
    grated finely
1 teaspoon finely chopped
    coriander root and
    stem mixture
1 teaspoon fish sauce
50g shelled cooked prawns,
    chopped finely
1 teaspoon cornflour
2 teaspoons water
12 x 12cm-square
    spring roll wrappers
vegetable oil, for deep-frying
cucumber dipping sauce
1 lebanese cucumber (130g),
    seeded, sliced thinly
½ cup (110g) sugar
1 cup (250ml) water
½ cup (125ml) white vinegar
4cm piece fresh ginger
    (20g), grated
1 teaspoon salt
2 fresh red thai chillies,
    sliced thinly
3 green onions, sliced thinly
1 tablespoon coarsely chopped
    fresh coriander

1 Place vermicelli in medium heatproof bowl; cover with boiling water. Stand until just tender; drain. Using kitchen scissors, cut vermicelli into random lengths.

2 Heat oil in wok; stir-fry pork, garlic and chilli until pork is changed in colour. Add onion, carrot, coriander mixture, fish sauce and prawns; stir-fry until vegetables just soften. Place stir-fried mixture in small bowl with vermicelli; cool.

3 Blend cornflour with the water in small bowl. Place 1 level tablespoon of the filling near one corner of each wrapper. Lightly brush edges of each wrapper with cornflour mixture; roll to enclose filling, folding in ends.

4 Make cucumber dipping sauce (freeze excess for a future use).

5 Just before serving, heat oil in wok or large saucepan; deep-fry spring rolls, in batches, until golden brown. Drain on absorbent paper; serve with cucumber dipping sauce.

cucumber dipping sauce Place cucumber in large heatproof serving bowl. Combine sugar, the water, vinegar, ginger and salt in small saucepan, stir over heat without boiling until sugar is dissolved; pour over cucumber. Sprinkle with chilli, onion and coriander; refrigerate, covered, until chilled.

makes 12 spring rolls and 1½ cups dipping sauce
per spring roll 3.5g fat; 279kJ (67 cal)
per tablespoon dipping sauce
0g fat; 107kJ (26 cal)

curry puffs

2 teaspoons peanut oil
2 teaspoons finely chopped
  coriander root
2 green onions, chopped finely
1 clove garlic, crushed
100g beef mince
½ teaspoon ground turmeric
½ teaspoon ground cumin
¼ teaspoon ground coriander
2 teaspoons fish sauce
1 tablespoon water
½ cup (110g) mashed potato
2 sheets ready-rolled frozen
  puff pastry
1 egg, beaten lightly
vegetable oil, for deep frying
sweet chilli dipping sauce
12 fresh red thai chillies,
  chopped coarsely
8 cloves garlic, quartered
2 cups (500ml) white vinegar
1 cup (220g) caster sugar
2 teaspoons salt
2 teaspoons tamarind paste

1 Make sweet chilli dipping sauce (freeze excess for a future use).

2 Heat oil in wok; stir-fry coriander root, onion, garlic and beef until beef is changed in colour. Add turmeric, cumin and ground coriander; stir-fry until fragrant. Add fish sauce and the water; simmer, uncovered, until mixture thickens. Stir in potato; cool.

3 Using 9cm cutter, cut four rounds from each pastry sheet. Place 1 level tablespoon of the filling in centre of each round; brush around edge lightly with egg. Fold pastry over to enclose filling, pressing edges together to seal.

4 Just before serving, heat oil in large saucepan; deep-fry curry puffs, in batches, until crisp and browned lightly. Drain on absorbent paper; serve with dipping sauce.

sweet chilli dipping sauce Place ingredients in medium saucepan, stir over heat without boiling until sugar is dissolved; bring to a boil. Reduce heat; simmer, uncovered, about 20 minutes or until slightly thickened. Cool 5 minutes; blend or process until pureed.

makes 8 puffs and 1½ cups dipping sauce
per curry puff 8.3g fat; 481kJ (115 cal)
per tablespoon dipping sauce
0g fat; 220kJ (52 cal)

fish cakes

500g redfish fillets, skinned
   and boned
2 tablespoons red curry paste
   (page 60)
2 fresh kaffir lime leaves, torn
2 green onions,
   chopped coarsely
1 tablespoon fish sauce
1 tablespoon lime juice
2 tablespoons finely chopped
   fresh coriander
3 snake beans (30g),
   chopped finely
2 fresh red thai chillies,
   chopped finely
peanut oil, for deep-frying

1 Cut fish into small pieces. Blend or process fish with curry paste, lime leaves, onion, sauce and juice until mixture forms a smooth paste. Combine fish mixture in medium bowl with coriander, beans and chilli.

2 Roll 1 heaped tablespoon of the fish mixture into ball, then flatten into cake shape; repeat with remaining mixture.

3 Just before serving, heat oil in wok or large saucepan; deep-fry fish cakes, in batches, until browned lightly and cooked through. Drain on absorbent paper; serve with fresh coriander leaves and lime wedges, if desired.

makes 16 fish cakes
per fish cake 2.8g fat; 201kJ (48 cal)
tip Fish cakes can also be sprayed on one side with cooking-oil spray and char-grilled, oiled-side down, on the flat plate of a barbecue for 2 minutes. Spray uncooked side, then turn and cook a further 2 minutes.

mixed satay sticks

250g chicken breast fillets
250g beef eye fillet
250g pork fillet
2 cloves garlic, crushed
2 teaspoons brown sugar
¼ teaspoon sambal oelek
1 teaspoon ground turmeric
¼ teaspoon curry powder
½ teaspoon ground cumin
½ teaspoon ground coriander
2 tablespoons peanut oil
satay sauce
½ cup (80g) roasted
    unsalted peanuts
2 tablespoons red curry
    paste (page 60)
¾ cup (180ml) coconut milk
¼ cup (60ml) chicken stock
1 tablespoon kaffir lime juice
1 tablespoon brown sugar

1 Cut chicken, beef and pork into long 1.5cm-thick strips; thread strips onto skewers. Place skewers, in single layer, on tray or in large shallow baking dish; brush with combined garlic, sugar, sambal, spices and oil. Cover; refrigerate 3 hours or overnight.

2 Make satay sauce.

3 Cook skewers on heated oiled grill plate (or grill or barbecue) until browned all over and cooked as desired. Serve immediately with satay sauce.

satay sauce Blend or process nuts until chopped finely; add paste, process until just combined. Bring coconut milk to a boil in small saucepan; add peanut mixture, whisking until smooth. Reduce heat, add stock; cook, stirring, about 3 minutes or until sauce thickens slightly. Add juice and sugar, stirring, until sugar dissolves.

makes 12 skewers and 1¼ cups satay sauce
per skewer 6.1g fat; 471kJ (112 cal)
per tablespoon satay sauce
5.5g fat; 278kJ (66 cal)
tip Skewers of meat and chicken can be brushed with combined garlic, spices and oil a day ahead and refrigerated, covered, until required. They can also be frozen for up to a month.

spicy sour prawn soup *tom yum goong*

900g large uncooked
  king prawns
1 tablespoon peanut oil
1.5 litres (6 cups) water
2 tablespoons red curry
  paste (page 60)
1 tablespoon tamarind
  concentrate
10cm stick (20g) fresh
  lemon grass, chopped finely
1 teaspoon ground turmeric
2 fresh red thai chillies, seeded,
  chopped coarsely
4cm piece fresh ginger
  (20g), grated
6 fresh kaffir lime leaves,
  shredded finely
1 teaspoon grated palm sugar
100g shiitake mushrooms,
  halved
2 tablespoons fish sauce
2 tablespoons lime juice
¼ cup loosely packed fresh
  vietnamese mint leaves
¼ cup loosely packed fresh
  coriander leaves

1 Shell and devein prawns, leaving tails intact. Heat oil in large saucepan; cook prawn shells and heads, stirring, about 5 minutes or until shells and heads are deep orange in colour.
2 Add 1 cup of the water and curry paste to pan; bring to a boil, stirring. Add remaining water; return to a boil. Reduce heat; simmer, uncovered, 20 minutes. Strain stock through muslin into large heatproof bowl; discard solids.
3 Return stock to same cleaned pan. Add tamarind, lemon grass, turmeric, chilli, ginger, lime leaves and sugar; bring to a boil. Boil, stirring, 2 minutes. Reduce heat; add mushrooms; cook, stirring, 3 minutes. Add prawns; cook, stirring, until prawns are changed in colour. Remove from heat; stir in sauce and juice. Serve soup hot, topped with mint and coriander.

serves 4
per serving 7.6g fat; 781kJ (187 cal)

chicken and galangal soup *tom ka gai*

3 cups (750ml) chicken stock
4cm piece fresh galangal (20g),
    sliced thickly
2 sticks fresh lemon grass,
    cut into 5cm pieces
4 fresh kaffir lime leaves
2 teaspoons coarsely
    chopped coriander root
    and stem mixture
500g chicken thigh fillets,
    sliced thinly
200g drained canned straw
    mushrooms, rinsed
1 cup (250ml) coconut milk
1 tablespoon lime juice
1 tablespoon fish sauce
1 teaspoon grated palm sugar
¼ cup loosely packed fresh
    coriander leaves
2 fresh red thai chillies,
    seeded, sliced thinly
2 fresh kaffir lime leaves,
    shredded, extra
1 stick fresh lemon grass,
    sliced thinly, extra

1 Combine stock, galangal, lemon grass pieces, whole lime leaves and coriander mixture in large saucepan; bring to a boil. Reduce heat; simmer, covered, 5 minutes. Remove from heat; stand 10 minutes. Strain stock through muslin into large heatproof bowl; discard solids.

2 Return stock to same cleaned pan. Add chicken and mushrooms; bring to a boil. Reduce heat; simmer, uncovered, about 5 minutes or until chicken is cooked through.

3 Stir in coconut milk, juice, sauce and sugar; cook, stirring, until just heated through (do not allow to boil). Remove from heat; stir in coriander leaves, chilli, extra lime leaves and extra lemon grass. Serve hot.

serves 4
per serving 22.8g fat; 1398kJ (334 cal)

crying tiger

50g dried tamarind
1 cup (250ml) boiling water
400g beef eye fillet
2 cloves garlic, crushed
2 teaspoons dried green
   peppercorns, crushed
1 tablespoon peanut oil
2 tablespoons fish sauce
2 tablespoons soy sauce
10cm stick fresh lemon grass
   (20g), chopped finely
2 fresh red thai chillies,
   chopped finely
1 large carrot (180g)
1 cup (80g) thinly sliced
   chinese cabbage
crying tiger sauce
¼ cup (60ml) fish sauce
¼ cup (60ml) lime juice
2 teaspoons grated palm sugar
1 teaspoon finely chopped
   dried red thai chilli
1 green onion, sliced thinly
2 teaspoons finely chopped
   fresh coriander
reserved tamarind pulp
   (see step 1)

1 Soak tamarind in the water for 30 minutes.
Pour tamarind into a fine strainer set over
a small bowl; push as much tamarind pulp
through the strainer as possible, scraping
underside of strainer occasionally. Discard
any tamarind solids left in strainer; reserve
½ cup of pulp for the crying tiger sauce.
2 Halve beef lengthways. Combine remaining
tamarind pulp, garlic, peppercorns, oil, sauces,
lemon grass and chilli in large bowl; add beef,
stir to coat beef all over in marinade. Cover;
refrigerate 3 hours or overnight.
3 Make crying tiger sauce.
4 Cook beef on heated oiled grill plate
(or grill or barbecue) about 10 minutes or until
browned all over and cooked as desired.
Cover beef; stand 10 minutes, slice thinly.
5 Meanwhile, cut carrot into 10cm lengths;
slice each length thinly, then cut slices into
thin matchsticks. Place sliced beef on serving
dish with carrot and cabbage; serve crying
tiger sauce separately.
crying tiger sauce Combine ingredients
in small bowl; whisk until sugar dissolves.

serves 4
per serving 10.9g fat; 951kJ (227 cal)

chicken green curry

¼ cup (75g) green curry
  paste (page 61)
2 x 400ml cans coconut milk
2 fresh kaffir lime leaves, torn
2 tablespoons peanut oil
1kg chicken thigh fillets,
  quartered
2 tablespoons fish sauce
2 tablespoons lime juice
1 tablespoon grated palm sugar
150g pea eggplant, quartered
1 small zucchini (150g),
  cut into 5cm pieces
⅓ cup loosely packed fresh
  thai basil leaves
¼ cup coarsely chopped
  fresh coriander
1 tablespoon fresh coriander
  leaves, extra
1 fresh long green thai chilli,
  sliced thinly
2 green onions, sliced thinly

1 Place curry paste in large saucepan; stir over heat until fragrant. Add coconut milk and lime leaves; bring to a boil. Reduce heat; simmer, stirring, 5 minutes.

2 Meanwhile, heat oil in large frying pan; cook chicken, in batches, until just browned. Drain on absorbent paper.

3 Add chicken to curry mixture with sauce, juice, sugar and eggplant; simmer, covered, about 5 minutes or until eggplant is tender and chicken is cooked through. Add zucchini, basil and chopped coriander; cook, stirring, until zucchini is just tender.

4 Place curry in serving bowl; sprinkle with coriander leaves, sliced chilli and onion.

serves 4
per serving 72.4g fat; 3826kJ (914 cal)
tip Remove any fat from the chicken thigh fillets before cutting them. You can substitute chicken breast fillets but they aren't as well suited to the robustness of the curry.

fish and potato yellow curry

8 tiny new potatoes
(320g), halved
400ml can coconut milk
2 tablespoons yellow curry
paste (page 61)
¼ cup (60ml) fish stock
2 tablespoons fish sauce
1 tablespoon lime juice
1 tablespoon grated palm sugar
800g firm white fish fillets,
cut into 3cm pieces
4 green onions, sliced thinly
⅓ cup coarsely chopped
fresh coriander
1 fresh red thai chilli, seeded,
sliced thinly
1 tablespoon fresh coriander
leaves, extra

1 Boil, steam or microwave potato until almost tender; drain.

2 Meanwhile, place half of the coconut milk in large saucepan; bring to a boil. Boil, stirring, until reduced by half and the oil has separated from the coconut milk. Add curry paste; cook, stirring, about 1 minute or until fragrant.

3 Add remaining coconut milk, stock, sauce, juice and sugar; cook, stirring, until sugar dissolves.

4 Add fish and potato to pan; cook, stirring occasionally, about 3 minutes or until fish is cooked as desired. Stir in onion and chopped coriander.

5 Place curry in serving bowl; sprinkle with sliced chilli and coriander leaves.

serves 4
per serving 24.2g fat; 2004kJ (479 cal)

pork jungle curry

2 tablespoons peanut oil
¼ cup (75g) red curry paste
   (page 60)
750g pork fillet, sliced thinly
⅓ cup firmly packed fresh
   thai basil leaves
40g pickled ka chai, sliced thinly
150g thai eggplants,
   chopped coarsely
1 medium carrot (150g),
   sliced thinly
100g snake beans,
   chopped coarsely
227g can bamboo shoots,
   rinsed, drained
2 x 5cm stems pickled green
   peppercorns (10g)
2 fresh kaffir lime leaves, torn
1 litre (4 cups) vegetable stock
4 fresh red thai chillies,
   chopped coarsely

1 Place oil and curry paste in large saucepan; stir over heat until fragrant.
2 Add pork; cook, stirring, about 5 minutes or until browned all over.
3 Reserve about four large whole basil leaves for garnish. Add remaining basil leaves, ka chai, eggplant, carrot, beans, bamboo shoots, peppercorns, lime leaves and stock to pan; bring to a boil. Reduce heat; simmer, uncovered, about 10 minutes or until vegetables are tender. Stir in chilli.
4 Place curry in serving bowl; sprinkle with reserved thai basil leaves.

serves 4
per serving 18.2g fat; 1601kJ (382 cal)

chicken panang curry

2 x 400ml cans coconut milk
3 tablespoons panang
  curry paste (page 61)
2 tablespoons grated
  palm sugar
2 tablespoons fish sauce
2 fresh kaffir lime leaves, torn
2 tablespoons peanut oil
1kg chicken thigh fillets,
  quartered
100g snake beans,
  chopped coarsely
½ cup firmly packed fresh
  thai basil leaves
½ cup (75g) coarsely chopped
  roasted unsalted peanuts
2 fresh red thai chillies,
  sliced thinly

1 Place coconut milk, paste, sugar, sauce and lime leaves in wok or large frying pan; bring to a boil. Reduce heat; simmer, stirring, about 15 minutes or until curry sauce mixture reduces by about a third.

2 Meanwhile, heat oil in large frying pan; cook chicken, in batches, until browned lightly. Drain on absorbent paper.

3 Add beans, chicken and half of the basil leaves to curry sauce mixture; cook, uncovered, stirring occasionally, about 5 minutes or until beans are just tender and chicken is cooked through.

4 Place curry in serving bowl; sprinkle with peanuts, chilli and remaining basil.

serves 4
per serving 82.1g fat; 4347kJ (1038 cal)

duck red curry

¼ cup (75g) red curry paste
   (page 60)
400ml can coconut milk
½ cup (125ml) chicken stock
2 fresh kaffir lime leaves, torn
1 tablespoon fish sauce
1 tablespoon lime juice
⅓ cup firmly packed fresh
   thai basil leaves
1 whole barbecued duck (1kg),
   cut into 12 pieces
565g can lychees,
   rinsed, drained
225g can bamboo shoots,
   rinsed, drained
3 fresh red thai chillies,
   sliced thinly

1 Place curry paste in large saucepan; stir over heat until fragrant. Add coconut milk, stock, lime leaves, sauce and juice; bring to a boil. Reduce heat; simmer, stirring, 5 minutes.
2 Reserve about eight small whole basil leaves for garnish; add remaining basil leaves with duck, lychees and bamboo shoots to curry mixture. Cook, stirring occasionally, about 5 minutes or until heated through.
3 Place curry in serving bowl; sprinkle with sliced chilli and reserved thai basil leaves.

serves 4
per serving 47.2g fat; 2408kJ (575 cal)

beef massaman curry

1kg beef skirt steak, cut into
  3cm pieces
2 x 400ml cans coconut milk
1½ cups (375ml) beef stock
5 cardamom pods, bruised
¼ teaspoon ground clove
2 star anise
1 tablespoon grated palm sugar
2 tablespoons fish sauce
1 tablespoon tamarind
  concentrate
2 tablespoons massaman
  curry paste (page 60)
2 teaspoons tamarind
  concentrate, extra
½ cup (125ml) beef stock, extra
8 baby brown onions
  (300g), halved
1 medium kumara (400g),
  chopped coarsely
¼ cup (35g) coarsely chopped
  unsalted roasted peanuts
2 green onions, sliced thinly

1 Place beef, half of the coconut milk, stock, cardamom, clove, star anise, sugar, sauce and tamarind in large saucepan; bring to a boil. Reduce heat; simmer, uncovered, about 1½ hours or until beef is almost tender.

2 Strain beef over large bowl; reserve spicy beef sauce, discard cardamom and star anise.

3 Place curry paste in same cleaned pan; stir over heat until fragrant. Add remaining coconut milk, extra tamarind and extra stock; bring to a boil, stir for about 1 minute or until mixture is smooth. Add beef, brown onion, kumara and 1 cup of reserved spicy beef sauce; cook, uncovered, about 30 minutes or until vegetables and beef are tender.

4 Place curry in serving bowl; sprinkle with peanuts and green onion.

serves 4
per serving 54.6g fat; 3688kJ (881 cal)

stir-fried seafood with basil

200g white fish fillets
8 mussels
250g uncooked king prawns
100g squid hoods
2 cloves garlic, crushed
1 fresh red thai chilli,
   chopped finely
1 tablespoon finely chopped
   fresh coriander root
¼ cup (60ml) peanut oil
100g scallops
2 tablespoons oyster sauce
2 tablespoons fish sauce
1 medium red capsicum (200g),
   sliced thinly
8 green onions, chopped finely
⅓ cup shredded fresh basil

1 Cut fish into bite-size pieces. Scrub mussels under cold water; remove beards. Shell and devein prawns, leaving tails intact. Cut squid into 6cm squares; score inside surface of squid using sharp knife.

2 Blend or process (or grind using a mortar and pestle) garlic, chilli and coriander until mixture forms a paste. Heat oil in large wok or frying pan; cook paste, stirring, about 1 minute or until fragrant.

3 Add all seafood to wok; stir-fry until seafood is tender and mussels open (discard any that do not).

4 Stir in sauces, capsicum, onion and basil; stir-fry 2 minutes. Serve with extra fresh basil and green onion curls, if desired.

serves 4
per serving 18g fat; 1406kJ (336 cal)

mussels with basil and lemon grass

1kg large mussels
(approximately 30)
1 tablespoon peanut oil
1 medium brown onion (150g),
chopped finely
2 cloves garlic, crushed
10cm stick (20g) fresh lemon
grass, sliced thinly
1 fresh red thai chilli,
chopped finely
1 cup (250ml) dry white wine
2 tablespoons lime juice
2 tablespoons fish sauce
½ cup loosely packed fresh
thai basil leaves
½ cup (125ml) coconut milk
1 fresh red thai chilli, seeded,
sliced thinly, extra
2 green onions, sliced thinly

1 Scrub mussels under cold water;
remove beards.
2 Heat oil in wok or large frying pan; stir-fry
brown onion, garlic, lemon grass and chopped
chilli until onion softens and mixture is fragrant.
3 Add wine, juice and sauce; bring to a
boil. Add mussels; reduce heat, simmer,
covered, about 5 minutes or until mussels
open (discard any that do not).
4 Meanwhile, shred half of the basil finely.
Add shredded basil and coconut milk to wok;
stir-fry until heated through. Place mussel
mixture in serving bowl; sprinkle with extra
chilli, green onion and remaining basil.

serves 4
per serving 12.2g fat; 877kJ (209 cal)

pork with eggplant

3 fresh red thai chillies, halved

6 cloves garlic, quartered

1 medium brown onion (150g),
     chopped coarsely

500g baby eggplants

2 tablespoons peanut oil

500g pork mince

1 tablespoon fish sauce

1 tablespoon soy sauce

1 tablespoon grated palm sugar

4 purple thai shallots,
     sliced thinly

150g snake beans, cut into
     5cm lengths

1 cup loosely packed fresh
     thai basil leaves

1 Blend or process (or grind using mortar and pestle) chilli, garlic and onion until mixture forms a paste.

2 Quarter eggplants lengthways; slice each piece into 5cm lengths. Cook eggplant in large saucepan of boiling water until just tender, drain; pat dry with absorbent paper.

3 Heat oil in wok; stir-fry eggplant, in batches, until lightly browned. Drain on absorbent paper.

4 Stir-fry garlic paste in wok about 5 minutes or until lightly browned. Add pork; stir-fry until pork is changed in colour and cooked through. Add sauces and sugar; stir-fry until sugar dissolves. Add shallot and beans; stir-fry until beans are just tender.

5 Return eggplant to wok; stir-fry, tossing gently until combined. Remove from heat; toss thai basil leaves through stir-fry.

serves 4
per serving 18.9g fat; 1387kJ (331 cal)

mixed vegetables in coconut milk

6 cloves garlic, quartered

3 fresh red thai chillies,
    chopped coarsely

10cm stick (20g) fresh lemon
    grass, chopped coarsely

1 tablespoon coarsely chopped
    pickled galangal

4cm piece fresh ginger (20g),
    chopped coarsely

4cm piece fresh turmeric (20g),
    chopped coarsely

2 cups (500ml) coconut milk

2 whole fresh kaffir lime leaves

4 medium zucchini (480g),
    chopped coarsely

6 yellow patty-pan squash
    (240g), chopped coarsely

200g cauliflower florets

100g baby corn, halved
    lengthways

2 tablespoons soy sauce

2 tablespoons lime juice

⅓ cup coarsely chopped
    fresh thai basil

2 fresh kaffir lime leaves,
    shredded finely, extra

1 Blend or process (or grind using mortar and pestle) garlic, chilli, lemon grass, galangal, ginger and turmeric until mixture forms a paste.

2 Place half of the coconut milk in wok or large saucepan; bring to a boil. Add garlic paste; whisk over high heat until smooth. Reduce heat, add remaining coconut milk and whole lime leaves; simmer, stirring, until coconut milk mixture thickens slightly.

3 Add zucchini, squash, cauliflower and corn; bring to a boil. Reduce heat; simmer, uncovered, about 5 minutes or until vegetables are just tender. Remove from heat; remove and discard whole lime leaves. Stir sauce, juice and basil into vegetable mixture; serve topped with extra lime leaves.

serves 4
per serving 26.9g fat; 1406kJ (336 cal)

stir-fried eggplant tofu

1 large eggplant (400g)
300g fresh firm silken tofu
1 medium brown onion (150g)
2 tablespoons peanut oil
1 clove garlic, crushed
2 fresh red thai chillies,
   sliced thinly
1 tablespoon grated palm sugar
850g gai larn, chopped coarsely
2 tablespoons lime juice
⅓ cup (80ml) soy sauce
⅓ cup coarsely chopped
   fresh thai basil

1 Cut unpeeled eggplant in half lengthways; cut each half into thin slices. Place eggplant in colander, sprinkle with salt; stand 30 minutes.
2 Meanwhile, pat tofu all over with absorbent paper; cut into 2cm squares. Spread tofu, in single layer, on absorbent-paper-lined tray; cover tofu with more absorbent paper, stand at least 10 minutes.
3 Cut onion in half, then cut each half into thin even-size wedges. Rinse eggplant under cold water; pat dry with absorbent paper.
4 Heat oil in wok; stir-fry onion, garlic and chilli until onion softens. Add sugar; stir-fry until dissolved. Add eggplant; stir-fry, 1 minute. Add gai larn; stir-fry until just wilted. Add tofu, juice and sauce; stir-fry, tossing gently until combined. Remove from heat; toss basil through stir-fry.

serves 4
per serving 15.2g fat; 1071kJ (256 cal)

chicken larb

2 tablespoons peanut oil
5cm stick (10g) fresh lemon
  grass, chopped finely
2 fresh red thai chillies, seeded,
  chopped finely
1 clove garlic, crushed
4cm piece fresh ginger
  (20g), grated
750g chicken mince
4 kaffir lime leaves
1 tablespoon fish sauce
⅓ cup (80ml) lime juice
1 medium white onion (150g),
  sliced thinly
1 cup loosely packed
  fresh coriander
1¼ cups (100g) bean sprouts,
  tips trimmed
½ cup loosely packed fresh
  thai basil
½ cup loosely packed fresh
  vietnamese mint
100g watercress
1 lebanese cucumber (130g),
  sliced thinly
1 tablespoon finely chopped
  fresh vietnamese mint, extra

1 Heat half of the oil in large saucepan; cook lemon grass, chilli, garlic and ginger, stirring, until fragrant. Add chicken; cook, stirring, about 10 minutes or until cooked through.
2 Add torn lime leaves, half of the sauce and half of the juice; cook, stirring, 5 minutes.
3 Combine onion, coriander, sprouts, basil, mint, watercress and cucumber in large bowl. Drizzle with combined remaining oil, sauce and juice; toss salad mixture gently.
4 Place salad mixture on serving plate; top with chicken mixture. Sprinkle with extra mint.

serves 4
per serving 17.7g fat; 1446kJ (346 cal)
tip Add minced chicken to pan in batches, stirring between additions, so chicken doesn't clump. Beef or pork mince can be substituted for chicken, if preferred.

char-grilled beef salad

This is a loose interpretation of one of our favourite Thai dishes, yum nuah, and is a good introduction to the flavours of South-East Asian cuisine. Rib-eye, boneless sirloin or eye fillet steaks are all good substitutes for rump in this recipe.

600g piece beef rump steak
2 teaspoons sesame oil
⅓ cup (80ml) kecap manis
1 cup loosely packed fresh
    mint leaves
1 cup loosely packed fresh
    coriander leaves
½ cup loosely packed fresh
    thai basil leaves
6 green onions, sliced thinly
5 shallots (60g), sliced thinly
250g cherry tomatoes, halved
1 telegraph cucumber (400g),
    seeded, sliced thinly
10 fresh kaffir lime leaves,
    shredded finely
100g mesclun
sweet and sour dressing
½ cup (125ml) lime juice
¼ cup (60ml) fish sauce
2 teaspoons sugar
2 fresh red thai chillies,
    sliced thinly

1 Place steak in shallow dish; brush all over with combined oil and kecap manis. Cover; refrigerate 30 minutes.

2 Meanwhile, combine herbs, onion, shallot, tomato and cucumber in large bowl; toss gently to combine.

3 Make sweet and sour dressing.

4 Cook steak on heated oiled grill plate (or grill or barbecue) until charred lightly and cooked as desired. Stand, covered, 10 minutes; slice thinly.

5 Place steak, lime leaves and mesclun in large bowl with herb mixture. Add sweet and sour dressing; toss gently to combine.

sweet and sour dressing Combine ingredients in screw-top jar; shake well.

serves 4
per serving 12.8g fat; 1275kJ (305 cal)

green papaya salad

100g snake beans
850g green papaya
250g cherry tomatoes,
  quartered
3 fresh green thai chillies,
  seeded, chopped finely
2 tablespoons finely chopped
  dried shrimp
¼ cup (60ml) lime juice
1 tablespoon fish sauce
1 tablespoon grated palm sugar
2 cloves garlic, crushed
¼ cup coarsely chopped
  fresh coriander
2 cups (120g) finely shredded
  iceberg lettuce
⅓ cup (50g) coarsely chopped
  roasted unsalted peanuts

1 Cut beans into 5cm pieces; cut pieces in half lengthways. Boil, steam or microwave beans until just tender; drain. Rinse immediately under cold water; drain.
2 Meanwhile, peel papaya. Quarter lengthways, remove seeds; grate papaya coarsely.
3 Place papaya and beans in large bowl with tomato, chilli and shrimp. Add combined juice, sauce, sugar, garlic and half of the coriander; toss gently to combine.
4 Place lettuce on serving plates; spoon papaya salad over lettuce, sprinkle with nuts and remaining coriander.

serves 4
per serving 7g fat; 677kJ (162 cal)

cold prawn salad

1kg large cooked king prawns
200g bean thread noodles
1 clove garlic, crushed
2 tablespoons fish sauce
1 tablespoon lime juice
2 teaspoons peanut oil
¼ cup (35g) coarsely chopped roasted unsalted peanuts
2 green onions, sliced thinly
¼ cup coarsely chopped fresh coriander
2 fresh red thai chillies, seeded, sliced thinly

1 Shell and devein prawns, leaving tails intact.
2 Place noodles in large heatproof bowl; cover with boiling water. Stand until just tender; drain. Using kitchen scissors, cut noodles into random lengths.
3 Whisk garlic, sauce, juice and oil in large bowl to combine.
4 Add noodles to bowl with nuts, onion, coriander, chilli and prawns; toss gently to combine.

serves 4
per serving 7.8g fat; 1353kJ (323 cal)

pomelo salad

1 small red onion (100g)
4 large pomelos (4kg)
2 green onions, sliced thinly
2 fresh red thai chillies, sliced thinly
¼ cup coarsely chopped fresh coriander
½ cup (70g) coarsely chopped roasted unsalted peanuts
2 cloves garlic, crushed
1 tablespoon grated palm sugar
¼ cup (60ml) lime juice
1 tablespoon soy sauce

1 Halve red onion; cut each half into paper-thin wedges.
2 Peel and carefully segment pomelos; discard
membranes. Combine segments in large bowl
with onions, chilli, coriander and nuts.
3 Combine remaining ingredients in small jug; stir
until sugar dissolves. Pour dressing over pomelo
mixture; toss gently to combine.

serves 4
per serving 10.6g fat; 1311kJ (313 cal)

yellow coconut rice

1¾ cups (350g) long-grain white rice
1¼ cups (310ml) water
400ml can coconut cream
½ teaspoon salt
1 teaspoon sugar
½ teaspoon ground turmeric
pinch saffron threads

1 Soak rice in large bowl of cold water for 30 minutes.
Pour rice into strainer; rinse under cold water until
water runs clear. Drain.
2 Place rice and remaining ingredients in large
heavy-based saucepan; cover, bring to a boil, stirring
occasionally. Reduce heat; simmer, covered, about
15 minutes or until rice is tender. Remove from heat;
stand, covered, 5 minutes.

serves 4
per serving 21.1g fat; 2167kJ (518 cal)

chicken and thai basil fried rice

¼ cup (60ml) peanut oil
1 medium brown onion (150g), chopped finely
3 cloves garlic, crushed
2 fresh green thai chillies, seeded, chopped finely
1 tablespoon brown sugar
500g chicken breast fillets, chopped coarsely
2 medium red capsicums (400g), sliced thinly
200g green beans, chopped coarsely
4 cups cooked jasmine rice
2 tablespoons fish sauce
2 tablespoons soy sauce
½ cup loosely packed fresh thai basil leaves

1 Heat oil in wok; stir-fry onion, garlic and chilli until onion softens. Add sugar; stir-fry until dissolved. Add chicken; stir-fry until lightly browned. Add capsicum and beans; stir-fry until vegetables are just tender and chicken is cooked through.
2 Add rice and sauces; stir-fry, tossing gently to combine. Remove from heat; add basil leaves, toss gently to combine.

serves 4
per serving 21.7g fat; 1922kJ (459 cal)

fried rice stick noodles *pad thai*

40g tamarind pulp

½ cup (125ml) boiling water

2 tablespoons grated
   palm sugar

⅓ cup (80ml) sweet chilli sauce

⅓ cup (80ml) fish sauce

375g rice stick noodles

12 medium uncooked
   prawns (500g)

2 cloves garlic, crushed

2 tablespoons finely chopped
   preserved turnip

2 tablespoons dried shrimp

4cm piece fresh ginger
   (20g), grated

2 fresh red thai chillies, seeded,
   chopped coarsely

1 tablespoon peanut oil

250g pork mince

3 eggs, beaten lightly

2 cups (160g) bean sprouts

4 green onions, sliced thinly

⅓ cup coarsely chopped
   fresh coriander

¼ cup (35g) coarsely chopped
   roasted unsalted peanuts

1 lime, quartered

1 Soak tamarind pulp in the boiling water for 30 minutes. Pour tamarind into fine strainer over small bowl; push as much tamarind pulp through strainer as possible, scraping underside of strainer occasionally. Discard any tamarind solids left in strainer; reserve pulp liquid in bowl. Mix sugar and sauces into bowl with tamarind; reserve.

2 Meanwhile, place noodles in large heatproof bowl; cover with boiling water, stand until noodles just soften, drain.

3 Shell and devein prawns, leaving tails intact.

4 Blend or process (or grind using mortar and pestle) garlic, turnip, shrimp, ginger and chilli until mixture forms a paste.

5 Heat oil in wok; stir-fry spice paste until fragrant. Add pork; stir-fry until just cooked through. Add prawns; stir-fry 1 minute. Add egg; stir-fry until egg just sets.

6 Add noodles, tamarind mixture, sprouts and half of the onion; stir-fry, tossing gently until combined. Remove from heat; toss remaining onion, coriander and nuts through pad thai. Serve with lime wedges.

serves 4
per serving 19.7g fat; 2576kJ (615 cal)

deep-fried noodles with chicken *mee krob*

vegetable oil, for deep-frying
125g dried rice noodles
1½ tablespoons peanut oil
2 eggs, beaten lightly
1 tablespoon water
500g chicken mince
¼ cup (60ml) lemon juice
2 tablespoons fish sauce
2 tablespoons tomato sauce
1 teaspoon soy sauce
2 tablespoons brown sugar
2 teaspoons finely chopped
 fresh red thai chillies
1 tablespoon finely chopped
 fresh coriander
3 green onions, sliced thinly
300g firm tofu, chopped coarsely

1 Heat vegetable oil in large saucepan; deep-fry noodles, in batches, until puffed. Drain noodles on absorbent paper.
2 Heat 1 teaspoon of the peanut oil in large wok or frying pan; pour in half of the combined egg and water. Swirl pan to make a thin omelette; cook until just set. Transfer omelette to chopping board. Roll tightly; cut into thin strips. Repeat with another teaspoon of peanut oil and remaining egg mixture.
3 Heat remaining oil in wok; stir-fry chicken until browned and cooked. Add combined juice, sauces, sugar, chilli and coriander; stir-fry 1 minute. Add onion, tofu and omelette strips; stir-fry until heated through. Just before serving, gently toss noodles through chicken mixture.

serves 4
per serving 29.1g fat; 2294kJ (549 cal)

crab fried rice in omelette

¼ cup (60ml) peanut oil
4 green onions, chopped finely
2 fresh red thai chillies,
    chopped finely
1 tablespoon red curry
    paste (page 60)
2 cups cooked jasmine rice
250g fresh crab meat
2 tablespoons lime juice
2 tablespoons fish sauce
8 eggs
2 tablespoons water
1 lime, cut into wedges

1 Heat 1 tablespoon of the oil in wok; stir-fry onion and chilli until onion softens. Add curry paste; stir-fry until mixture is fragrant.

2 Add rice; stir-fry until heated through. Remove from heat; place in large bowl. Add crab meat, juice and sauce; toss to combine.

3 Whisk eggs with the water in medium bowl. Heat about a quarter of the remaining oil in same cleaned wok; pour a quarter of the egg mixture into wok. Cook, tilting pan, over low heat until almost set. Spoon a quarter of the fried rice into centre of the omelette; using spatula, fold four sides of omelette over to enclose filling.

4 Press omelette firmly with spatula; turn carefully to brown other side. Remove omelette from wok; cover to keep warm. Repeat process with remaining oil, egg mixture and fried rice. Place omelettes on serving plate; serve with lime.

serves 4
per serving 26.3g fat; 1599kJ (382 cal)

curry pastes

With the exception of the massaman paste (which takes about 15 minutes to dry-roast the spices in a hot oven), these recipes only take a little cooking time, and will keep, covered tightly, in the refrigerator for up to a week. Each recipe makes 1 cup (300g) curry paste.

red curry paste

20 dried long red chillies
1 teaspoon ground coriander
2 teaspoons ground cumin
1 teaspoon hot paprika
2cm piece fresh ginger (10g), chopped finely
3 large cloves garlic, quartered
1 medium red onion (170g), chopped coarsely
2 sticks fresh lemon grass, sliced thinly
1 fresh kaffir lime leaf, sliced thinly
2 tablespoons coarsely chopped
    fresh coriander root and stem mixture
2 teaspoons shrimp paste
1 tablespoon peanut oil

1 Place whole chillies in small heatproof jug, cover with boiling water; stand 15 minutes, drain.
2 Meanwhile, stir ground coriander, cumin and paprika over medium heat in small dry-heated frying pan until fragrant.
3 Blend or process chillies and roasted spices with remaining ingredients, except for the oil, until mixture forms a paste, pausing to scrape down sides of jug occasionally during blending.
4 Add oil to paste mixture; continue to blend in machine, or using mortar and pestle, until smooth.

massaman curry paste

20 dried long red chillies
1 teaspoon ground coriander
2 teaspoons ground cumin
2 teaspoons ground cinnamon
½ teaspoon ground cardamom
½ teaspoon ground clove
5 large cloves garlic, quartered
1 large brown onion (200g),
    chopped coarsely
2 sticks fresh lemon grass, sliced thinly
3 fresh kaffir lime leaves, sliced thinly
4cm piece fresh ginger (20g), chopped coarsely
2 teaspoons shrimp paste
1 tablespoon peanut oil

1 Preheat oven to moderate. Place chillies in small heatproof jug, cover with boiling water; stand 15 minutes, drain.
2 Meanwhile, combine ground coriander, cumin, cinnamon, cardamom and clove in small dry-heated frying pan; stir over medium heat until fragrant.
3 Place chillies and roasted spices in small shallow baking dish with remaining ingredients. Roast, uncovered, in moderate oven for 15 minutes.
4 Blend or process roasted curry paste mixture, or crush, using mortar and pestle, until smooth.

panang curry paste

25 dried long red chillies
1 teaspoon ground coriander
2 teaspoons ground cumin
2 large cloves garlic, quartered
8 green onions, chopped
    coarsely
2 sticks fresh lemon grass,
    sliced thinly
2cm piece fresh galangal (10g),
    chopped finely
2 teaspoons shrimp paste
½ cup (75g) roasted
    unsalted peanuts
2 tablespoons peanut oil

1 Place chillies in small
heatproof jug, cover
with boiling water; stand
15 minutes, drain.
2 Meanwhile, stir ground
coriander and cumin over
medium heat in small
dry-heated frying pan
until fragrant.
3 Blend or process chillies
and roasted spices with
remaining ingredients, except
for the oil, until mixture forms
a paste, pausing to scrape
down sides of jug occasionally
during blending.
4 Add oil to paste mixture;
continue to blend in machine,
or using mortar and pestle,
until smooth.

green curry paste

2 teaspoons ground coriander
2 teaspoons ground cumin
10 fresh long green chillies,
    chopped coarsely
10 fresh small green chillies,
    chopped coarsely
1 large clove garlic, quartered
4 green onions, chopped
    coarsely
1 stick fresh lemon grass,
    sliced thinly
2 fresh kaffir lime leaves,
    sliced thinly
1cm piece fresh galangal (5g),
    chopped finely
¼ cup coarsely chopped
    fresh coriander root and
    stem mixture
1 teaspoon shrimp paste
1 tablespoon peanut oil

1 Stir ground coriander and
cumin in small dry-heated
frying pan over medium heat
until fragrant.
2 Blend or process roasted
spices with remaining
ingredients, except for
the oil, until mixture forms
a paste, pausing to scrape
down sides of jug occasionally
during blending.
3 Add oil to paste mixture;
continue to blend in machine,
or using mortar and pestle,
until smooth.

yellow curry paste

1 teaspoon ground coriander
1 teaspoon ground cumin
½ teaspoon ground cinnamon
1cm piece fresh turmeric (5g),
    chopped finely
5 fresh long yellow chillies,
    chopped coarsely
2 large cloves garlic, quartered
1 medium brown onion (150g),
    chopped coarsely
1 stick fresh lemon grass,
    chopped finely
2cm piece fresh galangal (10g),
    chopped finely
1 tablespoon coarsely
    chopped fresh coriander
    root and stem mixture
1 teaspoon shrimp paste
1 tablespoon peanut oil

1 Stir ground coriander, cumin
and cinnamon over medium
heat in small dry-heated frying
pan until fragrant.
2 Blend or process roasted
spices with remaining
ingredients, except for the
oil, until mixture forms a
paste, pausing to scrape
down sides of jug occasionally
during blending.
3 Add oil to paste mixture;
continue to blend in machine,
or using mortar and pestle,
until smooth.

index

conversion chart

MEASURES

One Australian metric measuring cup holds approximately 250ml, one Australian metric tablespoon holds 20ml, one Australian metric teaspoon holds 5ml.

The difference between one country's measuring cups and another's is within a two- or three-teaspoon variance, and will not affect your cooking results. North America, New Zealand and the United Kingdom use a 15ml tablespoon.

All cup and spoon measurements are level. The most accurate way of measuring dry ingredients is to weigh them. When measuring liquids, use a clear glass or plastic jug with the metric markings.

We use large eggs with an average weight of 60g.

DRY MEASURES

METRIC	IMPERIAL
15g	½oz
30g	1oz
60g	2oz
90g	3oz
125g	4oz (¼lb)
155g	5oz
185g	6oz
220g	7oz
250g	8oz (½lb)
280g	9oz
315g	10oz
345g	11oz
375g	12oz (¾lb)
410g	13oz
440g	14oz
470g	15oz
500g	16oz (1lb)
750g	24oz (1½lb)
1kg	32oz (2lb)

LIQUID MEASURES

METRIC	IMPERIAL
30ml	1 fluid oz
60ml	2 fluid oz
100ml	3 fluid oz
125ml	4 fluid oz
150ml	5 fluid oz (¼ pint/1 gill)
190ml	6 fluid oz
250ml	8 fluid oz
300ml	10 fluid oz (½ pint)
500ml	16 fluid oz
600ml	20 fluid oz (1 pint)
1000ml (1 litre)	1¾ pints

LENGTH MEASURES

METRIC	IMPERIAL
3mm	⅛in
6mm	¼in
1cm	½in
2cm	¾in
2.5cm	1in
5cm	2in
6cm	2½in
8cm	3in
10cm	4in
13cm	5in
15cm	6in
18cm	7in
20cm	8in
23cm	9in
25cm	10in
28cm	11in
30cm	12in (1ft)

OVEN TEMPERATURES

These oven temperatures are only a guide for conventional ovens.
For fan-forced ovens, check the manufacturer's manual.

	°C (CELSIUS)	°F (FAHRENHEIT)	GAS MARK
Very slow	120	250	½
Slow	150	275 – 300	1 – 2
Moderately slow	160	325	3
Moderate	180	350 – 375	4 – 5
Moderately hot	200	400	6
Hot	220	425 – 450	7 – 8
Very hot	240	475	9

Are you missing some of the world's favourite cookbooks?

The Australian Women's Weekly cookbooks are available from bookshops, cookshops, supermarkets and other stores all over the world. You can also buy direct from the publisher, using the order form below.

MINI SERIES £3.50 190x138MM 64 PAGES

TITLE	QTY	TITLE	QTY	TITLE	QTY
4 Fast Ingredients		Curries		Outdoor Eating	
15-minute Feasts		Drinks		Party Food	
30-minute Meals		Fast Fish		Pasta	
50 Fast Chicken Fillets		Fast Food for Friends		Pickles and Chutneys	
After-work Stir-fries		Fast Soup		Potatoes	
Barbecue		Finger Food		Risotto	
Barbecue Chicken		Gluten-free Cooking		Roast	
Barbecued Seafood		Healthy Everyday Food 4 Kids		Salads	
Biscuits, Brownies & Biscotti		Ice-creams & Sorbets		Simple Slices	
Bites		Indian Cooking		Simply Seafood	
Bowl Food		Indonesian Favourites		Skinny Food	
Burgers, Rösti & Fritters		Italian		Stir-fries	
Cafe Cakes		Italian Favourites		Summer Salads	
Cafe Food		Jams & Jellies		Tapas, Antipasto & Mezze	
Casseroles		Kids Party Food		Thai Cooking	
Char-grills & Barbecues		Last-minute Meals		Thai Favourites	
Cheesecakes, Pavlovas & Trifles		Lebanese Cooking		The Packed Lunch	
Chinese Favourites		Malaysian Favourites		Vegetarian	
Chocolate Cakes		Mince Favourites		Vegetarian Stir-fries	
Christmas Cakes & Puddings		Mince		Vegie Main Meals	
Cocktails		Muffins		Wok	
Crumbles & Bakes		Noodles		Young Chef	
				TOTAL COST	£

Photocopy and complete coupon below

Name _____

Address _____

_____ Postcode _____

Country _____ Phone (business hours) _____

Email*(optional) _____
* By including your email address, you consent to receipt of any email regarding this magazine, and other emails which inform you of ACP's other publications, products, services and events, and to promote third party goods and services you may be interested in.

I enclose my cheque/money order for £ _____ or please charge £ _____

to my: ☐ Access ☐ Mastercard ☐ Visa ☐ Diners Club
    PLEASE NOTE: WE DO NOT ACCEPT SWITCH OR ELECTRON CARDS

Card number | | | | | | | | | | | | | | | | |

3 digit security code *(found on reverse of card)* _____

Cardholder's signature _____ Expiry date ____ /____

To order: Mail or fax – photocopy or complete the order form above, and send your credit card details or cheque payable to: Australian Consolidated Press (UK), Moulton Park Business Centre, Red House Road, Moulton Park, Northampton NN3 6AQ, phone (+44) (01) 604 497531, fax (+44) (01) 604 497533, e-mail books@acpmedia.co.uk. Or order online at www.acpuk.com
Non-UK residents: We accept the credit cards listed on the coupon, or cheques, drafts or International Money Orders payable in sterling and drawn on a UK bank. Credit card charges are at the exchange rate current at the time of payment.
All pricing current at time of going to press and subject to change/availability.
Postage and packing UK: Add £1.00 per order plus 25p per book.
Postage and packing overseas: Add £2.00 per order plus 50p per book. **Offer ends 31.12.2007**